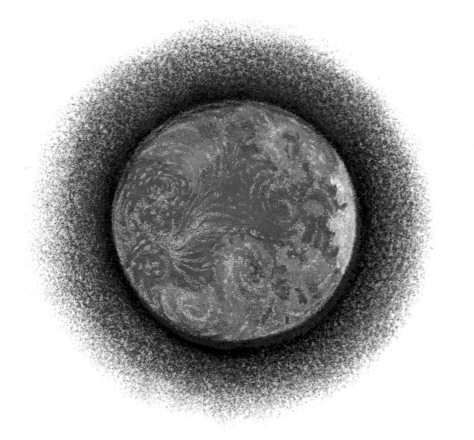

For Ted—L. M. S.

For Ed, who opened my eyes—B. B.

at the
bottom
of the
WORLD.

Layers of loose mud
blanketing the ridges and canyons
of the rocky crust

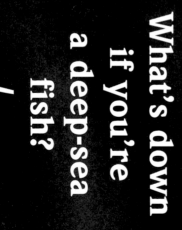

What's down
if you're
a deep-sea
fish?

Deep-sea fish flashing and flickering in the ink-black waters.

A sleek octopus
jetting toward
a hidden cavern.

What's down
if you're
an octopus?

An undersea park of giant sponges hosting creatures, large and small.

What's down if you're a sponge?

What's down
if you're
a ray?

A graceful ray gliding silently on wing-like fins.

Prickly sea urchins
dotting rocks like
black pincushions.

What's down
if you're
a sea urchin?

A ballet of seaweed twisting and twirling in endless currents.

What's down if you're seaweed?

What's down
if you're
a whale?

Rows of ocean waves,
swelling, surging,
splashing, crashing.

What's down
if you're
a wave?

A playful pod of
whales swimming
to their winter home.

What's down if you're a cloud?

Feathery, white clouds swirling over land and sea.

WHAT'S DOWN
if you're
the moon?

The pearly moon
hanging high,
reflecting soft, glowing
light into space.

What's up
if you're
the sky?

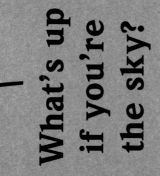

Bold, blue sky
wrapping the world
in fresh, clear air.

What's up
if you're
a bird?

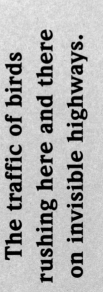

The traffic of birds rushing here and there on invisible highways.

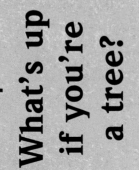

What's up
if you're
a tree?

Tall trees
spreading leaves
into umbrellas
of shade.

What's up
if you're
a butterfly?

Whisper-thin butterfly wings fluttering above petal cups.

What's up
if you're a
wildflower?

A sea of wildflowers
rising and falling
in tides of color.

What's up if you're a toad?

The trailing legs of a startled toad leaping out of sight.

Proud, new grass
pushing emerald
blades toward the sun.

**What's up
if you're the
grass?**

What's up if you're a root?

Loose, rich soil sewn together with thread-fine roots.

WHAT'S UP
if you're a mole?

Follow the arrows
and let your eyes travel up,
reading from the
BOTTOM of the page
to the TOP.

Then, halfway through,
turn the book around and
let your eyes travel down,
reading from TOP
to BOTTOM.

What's
Up,

What's
Down?

BY **Lola M. Schaefer**

PICTURES BY **Barbara Bash**

Greenwillow Books
An Imprint of HarperCollinsPublishers

What's Up, What's Down? Text copyright © 2002 by Lola M. Schaefer Illustrations copyright © 2002 by Barbara Bash
All rights reserved. Printed in Singapore by Tien Wah Press. www.harperchildrens.com

The full-color artwork was prepared with pastels on D'Arches watercolor paper. The text type is Weidemann Black.

Library of Congress Cataloging-in-Publication Data: Schaefer, Lola M., (date) What's up, what's down? / by Lola M. Schaefer ; pictures by Barbara Bash.
p.   cm.   "Greenwillow Books."   ISBN 0-06-029757-3 (trade).   ISBN 0-06-029758-1 (lib. bdg.)   1. Science—Miscellanea—Juvenile literature.
2. Upside-down books—Specimens.   [1. Nature—Miscellanea. 2. Upside-down books.] I. Bash, Barbara, ill. II. Title.
Q173.S287 2002 500—dc21 2001023895

1 2 3 4 5 6 7 8 9 10   First Edition